This book was presented to:

on this Day:

By:

Dear Creator

an anthology of hope & prayer
in word, image & song

by

Lynn Rose Curtin

and

The Pen Women of Jacksonville, Florida

Dear Creator: An Anthology of Hope & Prayer in Word, Image & Song

ISBN: 978-0-9893732-4-1

Editor: M.F.A. Shipp
Layout & Design: M.F.A. Shipp, Nada Frazier & Trish Diggins
Cover design: Trish Diggins
Spoken Word (CD): Lynn Rose Curtin, Sandy Hartman & Nada Frazier
Published by: Marcinson Press, Jacksonville, Florida
CD recorded & produced by: A1A Audio Productions, Mighty Music Group
CD cover: Trish Diggins

Created

This book was created by the Jacksonville, Florida Branch of the National League of American Pen Women, Inc. (NLAPW). The NLAPW was founded in 1897 and is the oldest non-profit, multi-disciplinary arts organization in the United States.

"Dear Creator" is an inspirational anthology of original invocations written and sung by Lynn Rose Curtin and supported by the artistic talents of branch members.

Once production costs are covered, proceeds and books will be given to non-profit organizations concerned with uplifting the human spirit. We see "Dear Creator" blessing persons in churches, hospices, homeless shelters, hospitals, recovery centers, and more.

Untitled, Duncan Sawyer

Dedication

This anthology is a compilation of select invocations and songs created by Lynn Rose Curtin while Chaplain of the Jacksonville, Florida, Branch of the National League of American Pen Women, Inc.

In addition, other members of the Branch have responded to Lynn's spoken and musical gifts with their own expressions of art, poetry, literature and photographic images, and contributed them to this volume.

We hope that these gifts will lift the hearts of all those who read these pages. We pray that they will inspire all those who listen to the CD of song and spoken word that accompanies this book.

About the Artist

Lynn Rose Curtin

Music and writing have been a significant part of Lynn Rose Curtin's life since she was a young girl. She started performing in coffee houses and supper clubs in the late Sixties, then went on the road in the Seventies singing countrywide in groups and as a single artist. She began using her music in the hospice environment throughout the eighties and nineties becoming a volunteer coordinator, and trained others to share music with patients and families, as well as doing in-services for the nursing and administrative staff.

Currently, Lynn is continuing to write music in the form of song prayers. She plays guitar, ukulele, piano and drums in churches, nursing homes, assisted living facilities, hospitals, and for individuals who request her music for their own personal healing. These song prayers are being recorded and will be available for individuals to use in hospice, churches, and individually. In addition, she is working on a collection of piano works.

Lynn Rose Curtin is a Letters member of the Jacksonville Branch of the National League of American Pen Women. Her lifetime of composition, performing, and spiritual musical expression are a reflection of her passion to be of service to others.

Frolic, Fur and Fun, Pat Setser

Untitled, Mary Ann Miller

Invocations and Songs

The Sycamores

Dear Creator,

The Sycamores have dropped their sticky seed pods and the holly berries are done falling on my walk. Now the trees stand in full adornment, all dressed in lush juicy green. It's Spring — the time to open our hearts to each other as the earth honors us with the opening of flowers, while cascades of color and perfume gift our senses.

Everything old is new again, inspiring fresh points of view. Many of us feel this rejuvenation and a recommitment to what brings us joy. We ask You to help us begin blooming in our own lives, and turning our thoughts and actions into beautiful gardens. We ask You to guide us in our journeys to a more positive way of being and seeing.

As we gather our thoughts like flowers, help us to share the ones that can make a difference in another's life and in our own. May those who need more beauty find it, and those who live in beauty share it.

Blessings to all those in need of more love and joy.

Amen.

Trees in Bloom, Pat Setser

Untitled, Duncan Sawyer

Shepherd of the Mountain

Dear Creator,

We offer this song/prayer
to the shepherds of our spirits and
those of all creation.

Shepherd of the mountain
Flower of spring
You both stand on the mountain
And you've seen everything
You stand in your silence
And you stand in your song
Your joy in each day
Slips in like the dawn

Play for me, play for me
A tune that's quiet and strong
And fills up the heart
With Spirit's song
Play for me, pray for me
Play for me, pray for me
Play for me, pray for me

Sing, Hey-ah, breeze of the laughing dark
Hey-ah, smile to our lonely hearts
Play for me

Shepherd of the mountain
In your holy space
With your newborn fawn
And compassionate face
You're the guardian light
The master of love
The keeper of dreams
The voice of the dove

Play for me, play for me
A tune that's quiet and strong
And fills up the heart
With Spirit's song
Play for me, pray for me
Play for me, pray for me
Play for me, pray for me

Sing Hey-ah, breeze of the laughing dark
Hey-ah, smile to our lonely hearts
Play for me
Sing Hey-ah, breeze of the laughing dark
Hey-ah, smile to our lonely hearts
Play for me, pray for me
Play for me, pray for me
Play for me, pray for me
Sing Hey-ah!

Amen.

Celebration of our Oneness

Dear Creator,

Today we gather in celebration of our oneness. As artists of many persuasions, we all confront the blank canvas, the clean sheet of paper, the unborn songs, poems, words, and visions that lie within our souls. We are grateful for the seeds of thought that allow us to bring our individual light into the world, so we can bring all who witness our creations into a collective circle. It is in this circle that we stand united in spirit and purpose - we stand in our strength and courage - we stand as one. So we continue to bless each other and we ask that special blessings be given to all those people and animals less fortunate.

Amen.

Beach, Mary Ann Miller

I've Come Home

I've been so long away
From the turning of the day
When Sunday mornin' came
And You were there to guide my way

We were young and we were old
We were sheltered from the cold
By the warmth of Spirit's light
We had more love than we could hold

I didn't know how much I missed You
Until I came around again
I walked inside to meet You
Just like a long lost friend
And I'm home
I've come home

Misty are my eyes
As I gaze up in the sky
And feel You watching me
Through the eyes of galaxies

We are one and we are two
With still so much to do
So I take You in my heart
To behold all that is true

And I'm home
I've come home
And we're home
We've come home

Summer Evening, Pat Setser

Let's Just Relax, Pat Setser

The Robins

Dear Creator,

The robins are here — flying in figure eights in front of our house, drinking from puddles in the road, resting in tree branches. So many robins. So much spring. Winter never really got started here and spring came eagerly bringing the promise of renewal, freshness, flowering gardens, and blooming spirits.

We thank you for the spring in our steps, the lightness of our beings, the feelings of hope. We thank you for these feelings reminding us of our freedom to choose who we want to be and who we are. We ask your guidance as we define our thoughts and deeds with the standards that speak to who we are as individuals. It is in our appreciation of ourselves and others that we can become full of heart like the robins are full of spring.

Please bless those beings who are less fortunate than we are. Thank you for listening to our prayers and our gratitude.

Amen.

Destiny, Suzanne Schuenke

Rainbow's Edge

Listening to the gentle rain
We feel the joy of spring
Gathered in our meeting place
You send us perfect grace
And on this rainbow's edge
Words and colors swirl
As we bring into being
What You place in our hearts

Dear Creator,
You give us everything
We need to make our world
So heaven lives on earth
We make our world
So heaven lives on earth

Breathing in Your energy
Peace comes and we go deep
Gratitude lights up our eyes
We feel our common ties
And on this rainbow's edge
Words and colors swirl
As we bring into being
What You place in our hearts

Dear Creator,
You give us everything
We need to make our world
So heaven lives on earth
We make our world
So heaven lives on earth
We make our world
So heaven lives on earth

The Ocean Breeze

Child, Mary Ann Miller

Dear Creator,

The ocean breeze lifts my hair into wisps of blowing salt air. There is a lightness of being here in the lap of Spring as I lean against the full belly of Summer. It won't be long now until Summer is born and Spring again fades into our memories.

We are all mothers. We have given birth to children, ideas, words, music, paintings, and even movement. We thank our Creator for sharing the gift of creation with us. This special time of year where a day has been chosen to honor mothers in our culture is a great reminder that each moment holds the potential for birth, no matter our age or place in the world.

So we thank You, Dear Creator, for giving us motherhood and for giving us each other.

Amen.

On Your Way, Pat Setser

On Your Way

In the wind along the Seine I see you
Floating on your boat into the sea

The breeze blows hard
and as you steer your moonbeam
I know you'll find the person you will be

All your life you've been a star
Shining bright from where you are

Now it's time to find your place
In a world that needs your grace

On your way, you're on your way
Oh, happy day, you're on your way

The sea and sky now hold your sails between them
You move beyond the skyline out of sight

When you return we'll all be here to hold you
And listen to your stories long and deep

All your life you've been a star
Shining bright from where you are

Now it's time to find your place
In a world that needs your grace

On your way, you're on your way
Oh, happy day, you're on your way

Thank You

part one

Dear Creator,

Thank you for bringing us together. Let us be mindful of the choice that is ours – the choice to make our every thought and action a living prayer of peace, filled with the light and energy to join the Divine with the ordinary. May the peace we feel within bring peace to the world around us. Today, this moment, let us be determined to think positively and be grateful that we have this precious time to make a difference, to make this world a better place because we are a better people.

Amen.

Untitled, Mary Ann Miller

part two

Dear Creator,

Thank you for bringing us back together today, and for guiding us to contemplate these words written by one of our greatest German poets, Rainer Rilke, who wrote: "be awake to the news that is always arriving out of silence." Let each of us be awake to this news arriving from silence, so that we may grab hold of that inspiration that is born from silence, that inspires us to paint, to write, to sing, to dance, to teach, and to connect with our creative voice. Let us take that voice and give it away to all we encounter along our pathways so that we may continue to enrich our lives and the lives of those around us through the experience of creative flow. Please bless our beloved Mother Earth and all her people and animals, and all soldiers in harm's way.

Amen.

Moments

Dear Creator,

We offer You this instrumental piece of music as we silently contemplate our relationship with You and with our world. We send You our deepest gratitude for the life You have given us and our earth and all her creatures.

Amen.

Blue Sky Cross, Nada Frazier

please see our Dear Creator cd for accompanying music

Reuniting Us

Dear Creator,

Thank You for reuniting us after our passage through the summer months. May our experiences of these months inform our direction as we go into the remainder of this year, enriching our contributions to each other and to our communities. As our soldiers continue to find themselves in harm's way, let us pray even more earnestly for peace in this world. And we ask that You watch with special care the people and animals less fortunate, while guiding us in the stewardship of our beloved Mother Earth. May we sustain ourselves by finding the Divine within all things, but most especially within ourselves.

Amen.

Poppy Field, Mary Ann Miller

Beach Fields, Mary Ann Miller

And So it Goes

I'm missin' the mountains and the cold crisp air
Missin' the tenderness of yesteryear
When life was so new and we stood in our youth
Rooted in our dreams and bound by our truth

Where are the friends that we held so dear
I don't see my face now when I look in the mirror
I remember my hometown in the aspen groves
Now nobody lives there but the creek that flows

And so it goes, we all grow old
We follow our dreams down that open road
And then one day when we reach the end
We become the songs in the blowin' wind

I've walked across sandbars and riverbeds
Picked up starfish and arrowheads
Everything old was new to me then
The sea and the earth became my dear friends

'Til I find the place where the mountains grow
And dance with the moon wearing leaves of gold
I'll be missin' the world that I used to know
And hearin' the voices from long ago

And so it goes, we all grow old
We follow our dreams down that open road
And then one day when we reach the end
We become the songs in the blowin' wind

And so it goes, we all grow old
We follow our dreams down that open road
And then one day when we reach the end
We become the songs in the blowin' wind
We become the songs in the blowin' wind

Dear Creator,

We know that life is a journey. We read about it, hear about it, and contemplate it. Today we share our realization of what it truly means to be who we are, how this world can be a better place.

Who We Are

We walk across the bridges
Leading over endless pathways
Headed for a meadow full
Of flowers wild with unborn days

And the rain turns the road into rivers
The fire sends its flame to the forge
And what we build is nothing more than
Who we are

We look into the gardens
With their laughing trees and flowers
And we dive into the ocean
With its hidden coral towers

And the visions outside our window
Dance like fire across the water
And what we feel is nothing more than
Who we are

Love is the sound in the starlight
It gave birth to you and to me
It's found in the wind and the ocean
It's the heartbeat of pure harmony

We go into the mountains
To find You in the forest shadows
The breeze brings Your voice inside us
As we recall love is all that matters

And the water falls like time on a dewdrop
The sun turns the grass to gold
And how we love is nothing more than
Who we are

Amen.

Butterflies and Flowers, Pat Setser

Butterfly Flowers, Nada Frazier

You are all I need

I want to sing You a love song
Give You all this life can give
Before I know my time is ending
I want to be the perfect me in You

You've always been where I'm going
Held me before I could fall
You put all my dreams into focus
So I could be the perfect me in You

I see Your light, I feel Your love
My soul is alive in Your creation
You're all I have
You are all I need

I don't need to look for a river
To take me away from the dark
With You there is a lightness of spirit
Now I can be the perfect me in You

You've always been where I'm going
Held me before I could fall
You put all my dreams into focus
So I could be the perfect me in You

I see Your light, I feel Your love
My soul is alive in Your creation
You're all I have
You are all I need

America, Susanne Schuenke

The Long Hot Summer

Dear Creator,

The long, hot summer is ending. We stand on the shore of juxtaposition as we look at each other today, September 10th, 2011. We remember tomorrow ten years ago as September 11th, 2001. We lost much then, and now we have opportunity to create from a different perspective, which comes from our ceasing to take time for granted. So we ask that we be given the strength to utilize our talents, and to honor each other in good and bad times. We ask for our hearts to continually fill with compassion. Bless all those people and animals who walk on dangerous pathways.

Thank You for listening to our prayers.

Amen.

Untitled, Duncan Sawyer

The Path of Days

My heart is filled with wonder as I hear Your voice
The owl and crickets tell me it's time to rejoice
I smell the tender blossoms of this summer's night
I lean into the darkness and begin to cry

And I pray You'll guide my way
Where should I go or shall I stay
When I have lost the path of days
Show me the road that I must take

My tears reflect the moonlight as I bow my head
And reach into my pocket to read what You've said
"Just listen to the breezes where the angels sigh
And you'll hear My blessings in the earth and sky"

And I pray You'll guide my way
Where should I go or shall I stay
When I have lost the path of days
Show me the road that I must take

And I pray You'll guide my way
Where should I go or shall I stay
When I have lost the path of days
Show me the road that I must take

When I have lost the path of days
Show me the road that I must take

Unnamed, Mary Ann Miller

Haiti

Dear Creator,

Thank You for bringing us all together in this first month of a new year. May we set our intentions with ease and grace, and direct our talents and creative energies into service to each other and to our communities. We ask that special blessings be given to the people and animals who are suffering so in Haiti. Guide us all in the most useful ways we can each contribute our resources where there is so much need. Help us to better honor our beloved Mother Earth as we continue to pray for peace in this world. May we sustain each other by finding the Divine within all things, but most especially within ourselves.

Amen.

Cosmology
Susanne Schuenke

Circles in Motion

It's a beautiful mornin'
It's a beautiful day
Sun's on the rise now
We're headin' your way

We've been walkin' in dream time
Over mountains and plains
Sailin' the oceans
We're headin' your way

What a heavenly notion
Circles in motion
Spinning through starlight
Everything so bright

Let us dance in the moonlight
Holding on so tight
Circles in motion
What a heavenly notion

It's a beautiful mornin'
It's a beautiful day
Sun's on the rise now
We're headin' your way

We see everything movin'
The stars fall and rise
Clouds full of spirit
We're headin' your way

What a heavenly notion
Circles in motion
Spinning through starlight
Everything so bright

Let us dance in the moonlight
Holding on so tight
Circles in motion
What a heavenly notion

Dramatic Sky, Pat Setser

Moving Faster Now

Dear Creator,

Another month has taken us further into this new year. Everything is moving faster now, yet it is in the slow walk of contemplation that we are able to slow our breath and open our eyes fully to the beauty all around us. The sunrise was so beautiful this morning that I wanted to know it could be held and made to last forever in an artist's craft. Then I thought about us. I look around this room at this moment and I see such artists, and I am honored by the gifts we have been given to capture the depths of life in all its beauty, joy, sorrow, and transition. May we take the responsibility that comes with these endowments and use them for the betterment of our world. We ask You, Dear Creator, to bless all the forms of life without vision or hope or love.

Amen.

Dawn, Susanne Schuenke

Dear Creator,

I look out the window and see children playing with their puppy in their yard — so sweet, so tender and innocent. And I am compelled to think about myself as I enter into another new decade far removed from childhood. Here we are today sitting around this table as friends and Pen Women. I know we are no longer innocent, but still we are sweet, we are tender, and we can also add that we are wise. Our prayer today is that we always find a way to maintain the childish wonder and sense of playfulness. We offer this poem to You and to each other:

Child Song

O day, when the dreams were long
And time was too short to remember
Nothing mattered but the sound of the rain
Falling on the first spring flower

The meadows were full of berries and sage
Blankets of juniper slept there
We ran in the forest that circled the lake
And lived in the hills of September

O day, when the seasons were friendly
And storms never came without reason
The stars were the seeds of the sun
And the grass was my soft bed of wisdom

As a child I found many treasures
Troubles belonged to the moon
I never moved faster than daylight
My life never ran out of room

Amen.

Spring in Georgia, Pat Setser

We Have Walked

Dear Creator,

We have walked through the endless fields of summer watching our dreams and creations bloom and prosper. Sometimes those buds don't open to us when we want, yet You remind us that all is in Divine order. We know this in the rise and fall of the tides, the moon's evolution across the sky, the rising and setting of the sun, birth and death. The rhythm is constant. May we be as constant in our journeys through the fullness of life. As the night grows longer now, may we be able to go deeper in our understanding of what we each harvest for ourselves and others.

Amen.

The Road to Yesteryear, Nada Frazier

Make A Wish, Nada Frazier

Wowicala
(Chant of Faith)

Wowicala, wowicala
Wowicala, wowicala
I believe in You
I do
I have faith in You
My God

Wowicala, wowicala
Wowicala, wowicala
I believe in You
I do
I have faith in You
My God

Wowicala is a Lakota Sioux word meaning 'faith'

In the Wind, Nada Frazier

Reflections

We respond in Love and Hope

Gingko, Susanne Schuenke

Love Within Us

A Reflection on "Who We Are" by Lynn Curtin

Faith is a mystery as we stand on the things we cannot see, listen to a voice we long to hear, and reach out to the Spirit within us.

We face the fire that leaps across the fortresses of our thoughts, dreams and hopes watching without warning the powerful flames that quickly reduce them all to ashes. Yet, Who we are is Who we are becoming. We will rise again, to seek love, embrace our passions and always believe someone out there is looking for us to fill in the emptiness of their own heart.

If love is the sound of starlight, then the visions outside our window must dance like fire that leaps across the oceans of our destiny.

How we love is nothing more than who we are... but Who We Are is Love Eternal.

Epiphany

There are times when sunrise dawns

Or sunset falls

Or late in fading afternoon

No bird calls

And nothing speaks

And whispering leaves are still

When in that sanctuary the pulsing shatter of creation

Scatters all the vision that we see

And through that silent rent in time

The beating heart of God fills all the heaven's vault

Its touch, alive, sublime, Divine

When all creation knows that it is one

So said John Muir and John James Audubon

So say Jane Goodall and Margaret Meade

So says the eternal wellspring of my soul

End of the Day, Phoebe Marner

Fall, Mary Ann Miller

Home

Home. Dorothy came to know there's no place like it. I believe that, too. I also believe it's not any place one can find on a map. Like Dorothy, we must look elsewhere.

Writers have often spoken of a sense of place. Well, there's a word: Sense. And that holds a key, for it is the sense of place rather than the place itself that matters. A sense of comfort, a sense of serenity, a sense of love, a sense of safety, a sense of endless imagination and pure being.

When have you found such a place? Where have you felt most at home?

Any hint of southern California draws me like a magnet to thoughts of my childhood home. It's still there and now shelters a hospitable mid-life couple who has restored it to its glory. I know because I took the opportunity to visit it several years ago, on my birthday, sixty-some years after I had last seen it. It snuggles beside the San Gabriel Mountains in Pasadena, just half a block off Colorado Avenue on which the Tournament of Roses parades every New Year's Day.

As part of our Elderhostel trip about all things Parade, on December 30 my companion and I had arrived at Pasadena Junior College to watch the competition of bands that would be marching down Colorado Boulevard two days later. We had been told to arrive at the college early to be sure of getting seats, so we did. We were over an hour early!

Now instead of sitting and waiting, something I don't do well, and knowing "my home" was but a few blocks away, with her blessing I took off, hurried alone down Colorado, turned onto North San Marino, and savored every step it took to reach the single-storied white colonial cottage that sat waiting. While time sometimes plays tricks with memory, I found it just as I remembered except for one thing: the front lawn had somehow shrunk.

Home. The same columned front porch stretches across its width. The front door stands midway, accented by the French doors on each side. The same two dormered attic windows watch as I approach. Once I identify myself and my reason for coming, the current mistress of the house invites me in. To my good fortune, she stayed home from work that day.

Leanne tells me how she and her husband came to own it. They had loved it at first sight in spite of its condition. Because they sensed it could be a wonderful home, she and husband Mark had purchased the place a handful of years before for a bargain $125,000 – rotted floors, punched-out walls, leaking roof, rats and all. They could restore it. They could do most of the work themselves. What I now saw proved them right.

Just as I had remembered, the front half of the rectangular layout left to right houses the living room. The fireplace still holds court on the end wall to the left, with the passage to the bedrooms and bath on the back wall.

Wooden floors gleam throughout. To the right of the entrance lies the dining room of equal size. With a door to the Pullman kitchen behind. The morning sun still peers in through the windows over the ample built-in china cabinet that is centered on the right wall. Again left to right, the back half of the rectangle houses what once was the master bedroom with its door to

the backyard, now their guest room. Then the bathroom, then "my" room. The door on the right connects to the kitchen. As we go from room to room, I recall aloud how each had been furnished so long ago. Leanne nods understanding. That they now use "my" room as the master bedroom seems right for this childless couple.

And now for the back yard, my childhood haven. I describe it in detail for my hostess. The yard had been bordered with fruit trees – apricot, kumquat, peach (under which my tent was pitched each summer) – and by the free-standing garage, a sturdy walnut tree that accommodated a crude child-made platform to perch on that reached to the garage roof.

Behind my parents' bedroom the huge apricot tree stretched its arms. Under it, Adirondack chairs lazed, from it my swing hung, and in its crook about eight feet skyward I had read many a book and dreamed many a daydream. One season the tree produced enough apricots for Mother and me to fill 56 Mason jars of the home-canned golden nuggets.

On the lush lawn in the center of the

backyard Daddy had perfectly lined a badminton court. It gave the three of us plenty of exercise. He transformed that court into a Victory Garden soon after the Japanese bombed Pearl Harbor. Tending it then became our exercise.

Neighbors came to admire some of its produce, especially his pet tomato plant with well over fifty fruits on it at one time. And how they puzzled over those curious fuzzy green pod things – something we called okra that were foreign to Westerners but that my very Southern Mother had to have to mix with onions and tomatoes and serve over rice. (Her sisters in Georgia sent us grits—an essential item in any respectable Southern kitchen--for even with all their wondrous variety, the western markets didn't sell grits.)

Home. Mother had an abiding sense that that was the South—though ironically her maiden name was West! While Pasadena was my childhood home, Savannah was hers. To her, Atlanta was the center of the universe. After all, she had been in the first Girl Scout Troop with Mrs. Lowe in Savannah. Moving to Atlanta in her early twenties, she was in the first group of licensed hygienists, and

Margaret Mitchell was one of her regular patients. So in the South she mentally lived and to the South she would in time return. Meanwhile in the west, at least she resided in a miniature Tara! And enjoyed okra! And served grits!

In addition to the okra that grew in the garden, Mother grew mint beside the back stoop, another hint to her leaning. She wasn't a writer, but she did have the same sense of place we know.

With all those memories flowing, I half-expected all to burst into vivid Technicolor as I now opened the kitchen door and stepped out.

But the yard was barren! Not a living thing, not even a sprig of grass. At least my apricot tree should be there, but no. The present owners had found the yard a-tumble and had upturned it all to begin preparing for a new lawn. Leanne, who grew up on a farm in the Midwest, gently explained that fruit trees have a limited life. No matter. To me the apricot tree still exists just as does Queenie, my collie – the first of many pets. As Hemingway is thought to have said, the best place for a writer to work is in his head.

So in my head I live and work on San Marino Avenue.

While on earth the Alcotts, Longfellow, Stowe, Twain, Wharton, Sendak, and Dillard identified with New England; Poe, Grey, Mencken, Millay, and William Carlos Williams with the Mid-Atlantic: Sandberg, Faulkner, Wolfe, Percy, Mitchell, and Mary Flannery O'Connor with the South; Cather and Sinclair Lewis with the Midwest; and Anais Nin, Frank Baum, Jessamyn West, London, Steinbeck, and Bradbury with the West. But in their minds they lived anywhere they chose – and shared, thank goodness, with us.

Hemingway apparently found the likes of home in Cuba and Key West, though in his case it somehow was not enough. So, like Virginia Woolf and Sylvia Plath and some other tormented souls, he chose to begin the ultimate journey on his own terms. Frankly, I think he went looking in the wrong place, or at least in the wrong way.

Home. Lynn, my Spirit Daughter, has been and continues to be the purveyor of so many wonderful songs – which she generously performs for many groups. It is her "I've Come Home" that inspired these thoughts of mine, as she has been inspired by the new spiritual home she has found. Her find has nudged me to move further along my own spiritual path.

As I stumble and plod on my way, I sense more and more that home is not a place in the West or over the pond or even beyond the rainbow. Instead it is within us, in our heads and in our hearts. The Creator has put us here a little below the angels and just a bit above the animals.

He has endowed us with flesh and blood for this life on earth and also with minds and souls to seek our eternal home.

While we cannot fathom His greatness or the plane on which He lives, He has given us an urgency to imagine and to offer up our gifts, whatever they may be, that we may come into His presence joyfully.

And so I know I must journey deep within myself and find a place to perch. My body is merely a cocoon which in time will open and fall away when touched by His grace. Then I will rise and I will soar with Him, for His Spirit leads me on and will guide me Home.

Love's Fragrance

Love is like a fragrant rose
Whatever shape or form
As solid as the first new bud
In the light of perfect dawn
And when the morning takes its flight
And noontime sets the stage
This rose unfolds its petals
On nature's scenic page
Then as the twilight lengthens
And darkness settles in
Its fragrance lingers in the air
To cheer our hearts again

© 2014 Jackie Hand

Framed Beauty, Nada Frazier

By Any Other Name
Nada Frazier

Author's Note:
This is a poem I wrote in my "early" Pen Women days that was the result of the poets in the group being asked to write a poem about an art work created by another member, be it a picture or sculpture or whatever. And Lynn's words, under "Celebration", (no. 3), brought this poem to my mind. Lynn thanks the Creator for bringing us together so we can "inspire each other, create together, and journey together.

It is in our journey together into the unknown worlds of the blank page and empty canvas, the unborn thoughts and images that lie ahead, that we find our mutual voices." When Lynn speaks of "unborn thoughts and images that lie ahead," I think of the lines from her poem "Who We Are" (no. 13): "[We are] Headed for a meadow full/ Of flowers wild with unborn days."

Creativity
or Everything's Coming Up Roses, after a painting by Sarabob Londeree

Roses and other hothouse flowers
Spring up on the sandy beach, as cool-looking
As the swatch of ocean behind them
You can feel the weight of the scent
They hold inside: a beautiful secret
About to be released.
Oversized, they dwarf the small dunes.
Outrageous,
Like Mother Nature's bold black stripes
On the white, horse-like body of a zebra
Or the more than Italian-Mannerist elongation
Of a giraffe's neck.
Perfect;
We wouldn't have it any other way.
Any minute now the ocean
Will begin to roar its approval.

© 2013 Dottie Burris

Born to Eternity

Pastel Sunset
Nada Frazier

I release you now
And beckon you to come and find me
As I brush away the echoes of sounds
That hold darkness and light in their embrace
Spring to fall to winter — sun up to sun down
Hushed by the passage of time
I am comforted by the touch of hands
That have touched the eon star walkers
Who tread among the black hole wilds of my destiny
I leave the earth now as I soar
Beyond the moments of sorrow and joy
Into the space before time begins and eternity ends
And I fly and I fly, becoming
And I am, I am
At last
I AM

Untitled, Duncan Sawyer

Incantation for Healing

Divine Love
Source of my soul
Come into my blood and bone
Heal me long
Heal me strong
Enfold me in your healing song

© 2011 Sandy Hartman

Seasons of the Heart

Oh, the doorway is round
And the doorway is square
And the door, it opens on everywhere;
And the place where you stop
Is the place where you start,
In the changing seasons of the human heart.
Turn your head, turn your head
And consider where you've been,
All the people that you've known,
All the places that you've seen.
And turn your heart
Turn your heart,
And look toward home again.
Oh, it's not too late
To turn your heart again.
The door is round when you're born,
It leads square to the grave,
And what's in your heart Is all you can save.

With empty hands do we come,
With full hearts we pray to go,
And the love we give is all the life we know.
Turn your head, turn your head
And consider where you've been,
All the people that you've known,
All the places that you've seen.
And turn your heart
Turn your heart,
And look toward home again.
Oh, it's not too late
To turn your heart again.
Oh, the doorway is round
And the doorway is square
And the door, it opens on everywhere;
And the place where you stop
Is the place where you start,
In the changing seasons of the human heart.

Blood, Sweat and Tears, Pat Setser

Contributors

Jan Atchley Bevan
*Love Within Us, A Reflection on
"Who We Are" by Lynn Curtin*

Dottie Burris
*Creativity, or Everything's Coming Up Roses,
After a painting by Sarabob Londeree*

Lynn Rose Curtin
*Dear Creator, Invocations & Songs,
Born to Eternity, with Sandy Hartman*

Peg Redding Hallam
Home

Jackie Hand
Love's Fragrance

Sandy Hartman
*Incantation for Healing,
Born to Eternity (with Lynn Rose Curtin)*

Fletcher Shipp
Seasons of the Heart

Artwork

Phoebe Marner
Mary Ann Miller
Pat Setser
Susanne Schuenke

Photography

Nada Frazier
Duncan Sawyer

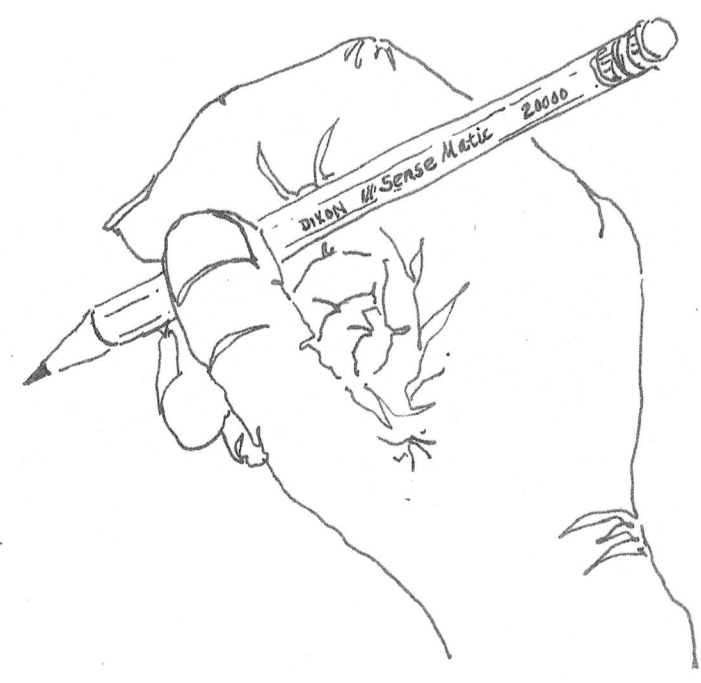

Hand, Mary Ann Miller

About Us

A Brief History of the National League of American Pen Women

The National League of American Pen Women, Inc. was founded in 1897 in Washington, D.C., as a reaction on the part of female journalists being banned from the Press Club, a section set aside in government offices for journalists to use. Three women took action following this unequal treatment: Washington journalist Anna Sanborn Hamilton, Emma Triepel, writer, and Mary Andrews Denison, a novelist. These women met at Mrs. Denison's home to discuss forming an organization that would bring together "women journalists, authors, and other illustrators for mutual benefits and the strength that comes of union."

From this meeting grew a core group of 17 selected women who gathered the following evening, June 26, 1897 to begin the preliminary planning. Three leaders emerged from this meeting — Marion Longfellow O'Donoghue, then a member of the Woman's National Press Association; Margaret Sullivan Burke, the first woman ever admitted to the Press Gallery, a political writer; and Anna Sanborn Hamilton herself, then social editor of the Washington Post. The women who gathered for this second meeting at Mrs. Denison's home were paid, published professionals and became the founding members of the National League of American Pen Women, which was legally incorporated July 14, 1897. By the end of that first year, membership had swelled to more than 50.

Membership continued to grow and spread throughout the states, until by 1921, it totaled 1,350. Today there are over 150 branches across the U.S., and more than 4,000 members. Pen Women are comprised of professional women in the fields of writing, art and musical composition — professions that traditionally live by their pens.

The Jacksonville, Florida, Branch had its birth in 1926 as the 31st Charter of the NLAPW, and sent one of its members, Margherita Gardner Fetter, to be the first Florida State President, serving from 1926 through 1928. The Jacksonville branch of the NLAPW is one of the oldest branches in Florida and currently has a membership of 28.

For more information, visit us at www.jaxpenwomen.com.

> Our national motto is One for All, and All for One.

In the Surf, Nada Frazier

For additional copies of this book, or to
purchase this book in bulk, please contact

The National League of American Pen Women, Inc.
Jacksonville, Florida, Branch
www.jaxpenwomen.com
or
Marcinson Press
www.marcinsonpress.com.

Find us on Facebook
www.facebook.com/dearcreatorbook
Also available through Amazon and Barnes & Noble.

CPSIA information can be obtained
at www.ICGtesting.com
Printed in the USA
BVOW07*2332150517

484200BV00003B/4/P